JUMPING SPIDERS AS PET

THE ULTIMATE GUIDE TO JUMPING SPIDERS CARE, COST, FEEDING, INTERACTION, GROOMING, HEALTH TRAINING AND MORE

PET TEAM WEES

Copyright© 2023 PET TEAM WEES

All rights reserved. No part or part of this book or publication may be reproduced, stored, or transferred in any form by electronic, mechanical, recording, or other retrieval system without written permission Of the publisher

CONTENTS

CHAPTER 1 5

   A Brief Overview of Jumping Spiders................................5

CHAPTER 2 9

SELECTING THE APPROPRIATE LEAPING SPIDER TYPE ...9

CHAPTER 3 13

CONFIGURING THE IDEAL HOME FOR SPIDERS 13

CHAPTER 4 19

   Guidelines for Nutrition and Feeding 19

CHAPTER 5 25

   Techniques for Handling and Interaction 25

CHAPTER 6 31

   Veterinary Medicine and Health for Leaping Spiders 31

CHAPTER 7 37

   Recognizing the Behavior of Jumping Spiders.................37

CHAPTER 8 44

TIPS FOR BREEDING AND REPRODUCTION 44

CHAPTER 9 ....**50**

DO-IT-YOURSELF SPIDER ENCLOSURE IDEAS 50

CHAPTER 10 ....**57**

TYPICAL OBSTACLES IN THE CARE OF JUMPING SPIDERS 57

CHAPTER 11 ....**64**

CONSIDERATIONS FOR SPECIES-SPECIFIC CARE........................64

CHAPTER 12 ....**71**

IMPROVING THE ENVIRONMENT FOR LEAPING SPIDERS.............71

BONUS CHAPTER **82**

FAQS 82

BONDING STRATEGY **114**

Chapter 1

A Brief Overview of Jumping Spiders

Scientifically categorized as members of the Salticidae family, jumping spiders are an intriguing and varied class of arachnids distinguished by their distinctive features and enthralling habits. Knowing the subtleties of these amazing animals as a potential owner is essential to giving them the best care possible and building a happy bond with your arachnid partner.

Unlike many other spider species, jumping spiders are known for having excellent vision. Their remarkable hunting abilities are partly attributed to their huge anterior median eyes, which are capable of perceiving both color and depth. These small arachnids show intellect and flexibility with a repertoire of fascinating activities that include precise jumping moves and complex courtship displays.

The manageable size of jumping spiders is one of the attractions of owning them as pets. These small animals, which usually have a length of 1 to 25 millimeters, are best suited for environments found indoors. Because of their small size, owners can closely observe the spiders' everyday activities, which strengthens the bond between the two.

Making a jumping spider's habitat suitable requires careful consideration of surrounding environmental elements. Their physical and mental well-being is enhanced by an enclosure that is well-ventilated, with suitable substrate, hiding places, and climbing chances, and matches their native habitat. For the spider to be comfortable and healthy, the temperature and humidity levels must be kept within the range specified for the species.

A vital part of jumping spiders' general maintenance is feeding them. These expert hunters, who feed on a wide range of insects, are carnivorous arachnids. Meeting their nutritional needs requires offering a varied food and making sure that feeding times are appropriate. Furthermore, providing live prey enhances their overall enrichment and encourages natural hunting habits.

Even though jumping spiders are typically low-maintenance pets, it's important for both the owner and the spider to understand safe handling practices. It is best to handle spiders carefully and gently while keeping in mind their behavior to ensure a favorable connection. Key factors in handling procedures are avoiding needless stress and showing respect for the spider's natural tendencies.

Veterinary care and health are essential components of conscientious spider keeping. The longevity and vitality of the jumping spider are ensured by routinely monitoring for indications of illness or stress and by seeking fast veterinarian assistance when required. Gaining knowledge about typical health problems and prophylactic actions helps the pet's general well-being.

Chapter 2

Selecting the Appropriate Leaping Spider Type

For any potential owner, choosing the right species of jumping spider is essential. Every species has distinct traits, needs for upkeep, and temperaments. Think about the following elements to help you make a decision:

1. Size and Appearance: Evaluate the physical attributes and sizes of various species. While some jumping spiders have distinct patterns, others have vibrant colors. Select a species that you find visually pleasing.

2. Temperament: Examine the personalities of different species of jumping spiders. While some may be more defensive, others may be more submissive and tolerant to handling. Match the spider's behavior to your degree of comfort and engagement expectations.

3. Habitat and Geographic Origin: Recognize each species' native habitat and place of origin. In confinement, emulating their natural habitat improves their quality of life. Tropical species, for instance, might need higher humidity levels.

4. Legality and Availability: Determine whether the selected species are allowed in your area. Furthermore, understand any legal limitations or prerequisites related to keeping specific species of jumping spiders as pets.

5. Activity Level: Take into account the species' level of activity. While some jumping spiders are more

sedentary, others could be more active, frequently hunting and exploring. Adjust the energy levels of the spider to the desired degree of engagement.

6. Feeding Requirements: Research the particular food requirements of every species. Certain jumping spiders might have more specific diets that call for a wide range of prey items. Make sure you are able to provide for their dietary needs.

7. Lifespan: The lifespans of many species of jumping spiders differ. Because many species can only live for a few months while others can live for several years, think about the commitment involved. Select a species based on your degree of dedication and lifestyle.

8. Information Availability: Choose a species for which thorough care instructions are easily accessible. In order to ensure effective ownership, having access to care

manuals, professional guidance, and community forums can be quite helpful.

9. Breeding Considerations: Learn about the needs and habits of the selected species if you're interested in breeding. Certain types of jumping spiders could require particular circumstances in order to reproduce.

10. Allergies: Keep an eye out for any possible allergies to the venom of spiders. Even while jumping spiders don't usually injure people, it's important to take individual sensitivity into account.

You may select the ideal species of jumping spider for your pet by carefully weighing these considerations. The world of spider keeping is enhanced by the distinct charm and individuality that each species offers its devotees, providing a wide array of alternatives to investigate and enjoy.

Chapter 3

Configuring the Ideal Home for Spiders

Your jumping spider's health depends critically on the creation of the perfect environment. To create the ideal home for spiders, adhere to these detailed instructions:

1. Enclosure Selection: Based on your jumping spider's size, pick an enclosure that is well ventilated. Use transparent containers so that they may be easily observed. Make sure there are no openings or gaps that could allow the spider to escape.

2. Substrate: Choose a floor covering that is appropriate for the enclosure. A peat-based substrate or coconut coir both function well as a stable, moisture-retaining

base. Enough depth to support web-building and burrowing activities.

3. Hiding Spots: Include hiding places in the habitat, including little huts, cork bark, or artificial plants. These areas offer a haven for rest and molting while simulating the jumping spider's native habitat.

4. Climbing Opportunities: Provide vertical climbing features like silk anchor points, tiny branches, or twigs. Because they are skilled climbers, jumping spiders can display their innate characteristics.

5. Humidity and Temperature: Sustain the proper amounts of both humidity and temperature. The temperature range in which most jumping spiders flourish is 70 80°F (21 27°C). It's important to take into account the humidity needs of certain species, as some

require higher amounts than others, particularly if they are native to tropical locations.

6. illumination: Give the enclosure ambient, indirect illumination. Because jumping spiders prefer shady regions, stay out of direct sunshine. A soft, natural light source helps create an atmosphere that is ideal for observation.

7. Ventilation: Make sure there is enough ventilation to avoid mold growth and stagnant air. The enclosure's top and sides have ventilation openings that allow air to circulate while preserving a steady atmosphere.

8. Prey Items: Take into account the jumping spider's dietary requirements. Make sure you have a steady supply of small, live prey such as little moths, pinhead crickets, or fruit flies. Providing a variety of prey enhances their diet.

9. Water Source: Set up a clean water source next to a tiny, shallow water dish. Steer clear of deep dishes to avoid unintentional drowning. Maintaining humidity levels can also be aided by misting the enclosure with water.

10. Environmental Enrichment: Add components for environmental enrichment, including tiny objects for exploration or silk strands for webbuilding. This promotes the spider's mental health and encourages natural activities.

11. Cleaning Schedule: Set up a regular schedule for cleaning to get rid of garbage, molten exoskeletons, and uneaten prey. A pristine habitat reduces the possibility of bacteria and mold growth and guarantees your jumping spider a clean and hygienic place to live.

12. Monitoring Equipment: To precisely measure temperature and humidity, get a thermometer and a hygrometer. Make sure these settings are regularly checked and adjusted to suit the unique needs of your species of jumping spider.

13. Prevent Escapes: In order to stop escapes, thoroughly inspect the enclosure. Make sure the lid fastens firmly and seal any holes. This keeps the spider from escaping as much and shields it from possible damage.

14. Maintenance Schedule: Create a schedule for routine inspections and updates to the habitat. This entails changing out the substrate, cleaning, and revitalizing the surroundings to give your jumping spider a continually cozy and engaging home.

15. Types of animalsParticular Aspects to Take into Account: Examine and put into practice any habitat needs unique to your species. Certain jumping spiders might require particular flora, microclimates, or substrate types. Make the habitat suitable for these subtleties.

By carefully following these guidelines, you'll create a setting that closely resembles jumping spiders' natural habitat, enhancing their health and happiness and enabling you to lead a meaningful life as a pet owner.

CHAPTER 4

Guidelines for Nutrition and Feeding

Your jumping spider's health and vitality depend on providing it with the right food and nourishment. Adhere to these detailed instructions:

1. Variety in Diet:

To satisfy your jumping spider's dietary needs, provide a varied food. A varied and well-balanced diet can be enhanced by the presence of adequately sized live prey items such as fruit flies, tiny moths, and crickets.

2. Feeding Pattern:

Depending on your jumping spider's age and species, change how often it eats. While adults can survive on a less frequent feeding schedule, juveniles usually need more regular meals.

3. Appropriate Size:

Give your jumping spider prey items that correspond to its size. Don't offer overly huge prey because it could suffocate the animal or hurt it when it's being fed.

4. Preference for Live Prey:

Choose live prey anytime it is available. Your jumping spider will engage in natural behaviors when hunting and catching live prey, which will stimulate its mind and body.

5. Extra Nutrition:

If you think that your prey items might be deficient in any particular nutrient, you might want to consider giving your jumping spider extra calcium in the form of powder or vitamin supplements. To determine the proper supplements, speak with a veterinarian.

6. Observation Throughout the Meal:
Keep an eye on your jumping spider while it is feeding to make sure the prey is successfully captured and consumed. If the spider appears uninterested or finds hunting difficult, you may need to modify the size or type of prey.

7. Source of Water:
Even though they get their moisture from their food, jumping spider enclosures should have a small dish of shallow water. Occasionally mist the enclosure to increase humidity and offer an extra water supply.

8. Times of Fasting:
Be aware that jumping spiders, particularly during the molting or reproductive processes, may experience

periods of natural fasting. Observe these times and refrain from trying to feed the spider more than is necessary.

9. Modifying the Feeding Program:
Adapt the feeding schedule to your jumping spider's degree of activity. Feed them more often when they're active, such when they're mating or creating webs, to meet their energy needs.

10. Freshness of the Prey:
Before giving live prey items to your jumping spider, make sure they are fresh. Nutrient-rich, vibrant prey adds to the hunting experience and is in good health.

11. Steer clear of overfeeding:
Take care not to give your jumping spider too much food. Obesity and other health problems can result from overfeeding. Depending on the age, degree of activity,

and general health of the spider, alter the amount and timing of feeding.

12. Keeping an eye on size and weight:
Keep a regular eye on your jumping spider's weight and dimensions. Substantial alterations could be a sign of nutritional needs or health problems. See a veterinarian if you observe any strange changes.

13. Strategies for Catching Prey:
Let your jumping spider use its natural means of capturing prey. Stay away from using forceps or any other tools that could agitate the spider. An integral part of their behavioral enrichment is the hunting process.

14. Regularity in Feeding Schedules:
Set up a regular feeding regimen. Regular feeding schedules assist to establish a predictable environment,

which lowers stress levels in jumping spiders, who frequently develop acclimated to routine.

15. Veterinary Examinations:

Make time for routine veterinary examinations to determine your jumping spider's general health. A vet that specializes in exotic animals can answer any dietary issues and offer insightful advice on your spider's health.

By adhering to these feeding and dietary recommendations, you'll support your jumping spider's general health, lifespan, and well-being and create an enjoyable and fulfilling experience for yourself as a pet owner.

CHAPTER 5

Techniques for Handling and Interaction

When handled and interacted with with compassion and understanding, caring for your jumping spider can be a fulfilling experience. To guarantee a fruitful conversation, use these strategies:

1. Calm Approach:

When interacting with your jumping spider, be calm and careful. Unexpected motions or disruptions may lead to tension. Approach the spider slowly so it can get used to you being around.

2. Hand Location:

To encourage a spider to voluntarily climb onto your hand, hold your hand out horizontally in front of it. Steer clear of abrupt movements and refrain from using force to pick up the spider since this may elicit defensive responses.

3. Hand Sanitization:

Be sure to fully wash your hands before handling the jumping spider. This ensures a clean and safe connection and reduces the possibility of passing any substances that could be detrimental to the spider.

4. Low to the Ground:

Engage in conversation near a level surface, such the floor or a tabletop. This keeps your jumping spider safe by reducing the possibility of unintentional falls.

5. Brief Meetings:

As the spider gets used to interaction, shorten the handling sessions and then progressively increase their time. Observe how the spider behaves and refrain from going outside its comfort zone.

6. First Observation:

Before you try to handle your jumping spider, observe it in its enclosure. Its comfort level and interaction readiness can be inferred from its behavior and disposition.

7. Moment of the Day:

Pick a time of day to handle your jumping spider when it is inherently more active. When a spider is molting or going through other delicate times, try not to disturb it.

8. Steer clear of abrupt movements:

Reduce the amount of loud noises and abrupt movements during handling. Because jumping spiders are vibration-sensitive, sudden movements may set them on the defensive.

9. Building Trust and Being Patient:

Develop trust gradually by interacting with others patiently and consistently. Your jumping spider is more likely to acquire accustomed to the handling procedure if it links handling with pleasant memories.

10. Honor Stress-Related Signs:

Pay attention to any symptoms of stress, such as jerky movements or erect legs. Give your jumping spider some time to adjust to its new environment and return it to its habitat gently if it shows signs of discomfort.

11. Employ a Gentle Bristle Brush:

If you find it difficult to handle the spider with your hands, you might try encouraging it to come onto your hand willingly with a small, soft brush. This approach reduces direct contact and may make the spider feel less threatened.

12. Steer clear of handling when molting:

You should not handle your jumping spider while it is molting. Spiders are very fragile during their molting period, and any disruption could be harmful to their well-being.

13. Developing a Bond via Observation:

Observe your jumping spider frequently to build a bond. Although touching can be helpful, some spiders might rather be watched than touched. Honor each person's unique preferences.

14. Employ a Catch Cup for Moving:

If you must move your leaping spider, avoid direct handling and instead use a soft brush or a capture cup. This eases tension and makes a calm, delicate transfer possible.

15. Age-Related Issues:

When deciding how frequently to handle your jumping spider, take its age into account. Adult spiders may be more tolerant of human contact, whilst younger spiders may be more shy. Make the appropriate adjustments to your strategy.

A great interaction experience and a stronger link between you and your arachnid partner are ensured when handling is done with compassion and respect for your jumping spider's natural tendencies.

CHAPTER 6

Veterinary Medicine and Health for Leaping Spiders

Even while jumping spiders can withstand a lot, it is still important to give them careful medical attention. The following rules apply to health and veterinary care:

1. Consistent Observation:

Make frequent notes about your jumping spider. Keep an eye on its food schedule, degree of activity, and any behavioral or physical changes. For health management to be effective, problems must be detected early.

2. Indices of Illness:

Watch out for symptoms of sickness, such as lethargy, altered appetite, irregularities in webbuilding, or peculiar body marks. Any departure from typical behavior or appearance has to be investigated further.

3. Molting Procedure:

Be mindful of the molting process. During molting, provide a calm and safe environment because any interruptions during this delicate time can cause problems. Make sure it's humid enough to facilitate molting.

4. Getting Alone to Molt:

If possible, try to keep your jumping spider alone during its molting period to ease its stress levels and lower the possibility of damage from other residents or disruptions.

5. Cleaning and Hygiene:

In order to avoid bacterial or fungal illnesses, keep the enclosure clean. Take out any garbage, molten exoskeletons, and uneaten prey on a regular basis. Maintain fresh substrate and swap it out as necessary.

6. Veterinary Advice:

Should you notice any recurring health issues or alterations in behavior, seek advice from a veterinarian who specializes in exotic animals. A specialist can offer advice and even perform tests to determine the health of your spider.

7. Preventing Parasites:

Take preventative measures to avoid parasites. Refrain from introducing wild-caught food because it could infect your jumping spider with parasites. Continue using a trustworthy source for captive-bred prey.

8. New Items in Quarantine:

Before introducing new jumping spiders to your collection's current residents, place them in quarantine.

By taking this precaution, possible infections are kept from spreading.

9. Control of Temperature:

Make sure the enclosure stays consistently warm, but not too hot, for the species of jumping spider that you have. Frequent variations may cause the spider to get stressed and weaken its defenses.

10. Issues with the Respiratory System:

Keep an eye out for respiratory symptoms like hard breathing or heavy fluid discharge. Sustain appropriate ventilation and swiftly attend to any issues to avoid respiratory discomfort.

11. Evaluation of Injury:

In case you think the spider is injured from a fall or any other incident, examine it closely. Small wounds might heal with time and in a stress-free setting, but if in doubt, get expert help from a veterinarian.

12. Determine Exogenous Parasites:

Look for outside parasites, including mites. Problems could be indicated by the spider rubbing against objects, scratching excessively, or having obvious parasites on its body. See a veterinarian to determine the best course of action.

13. Modifications in Behavior:

Keep an eye out for changes in behavior. Unusual webbuilding habits, an abrupt shift in activity level, or a lack of appetite might all be signs of underlying health problems.

14. Dental Infections:

Keep an eye out for symptoms of oral infections, such as redness or swelling around the mouth's edges. Any irregularities in the way the spider feeds could also be a sign of dental health issues.

15. Maintaining Records:

Observe your jumping spider's behavior and overall health. Feeding patterns, molting dates, and any noticeable changes should be noted since these might provide you and your veterinarian important information.

You may guarantee a healthy and happy life for your arachnid buddy and contribute to the general well-being of your jumping spider by implementing these health and veterinary care methods.

CHAPTER 7

Recognizing the Behavior of Jumping Spiders

Creating an environment that is both beneficial and rewarding for your pet requires an understanding of the behavior of jumping spiders. Here are some observations about their actions:

1. Astute Perception Techniques:
Jumping spiders have quite good vision, especially with their huge anterior median eyes. This enables them to precisely observe and track prey. They are inquisitive beings that pay close attention to their environment.

2. Methods of Hunting:
Spiders that jump are expert hunters. To catch prey, they use stalking and leaping techniques. Their ability to

jump precisely and their use of silk draglines help them navigate their surroundings and catch microscopic insects.

3. Production of Silk:

Although they don't build large webs like other spider species, jumping spiders employ silk for a variety of uses. They construct little retreats, use silk in courting rituals, and make draglines for protection during leaps.

4. Displays of Courtship:

To entice females, male jumping spiders perform intricate courtship rituals. These performances frequently feature complex motions, vibrations, and the application of vivid body paint. Your appreciation of their mating rituals is enhanced when you comprehend their activities.

5. Social Organization:

Most jumping spiders are lone individuals. They don't display social activities such as creating community webs, which some other species of spiders do. Usually, each spider guards its own region.

6. Molting Procedure:
Molting is a process by which jumping spiders grow and lose their exoskeletons. For spiders, the molting process is a delicate time that calls for a calm and safe space. For extra nourishment, they could consume their molted exoskeleton.

7. Vibration-Based Communication:
Vibrations are a means of communication for jumping spiders and are involved in interactions and courtship. They may add another level to their communication strategies by using substrate vibrations to signal to rivals or possible mates.

8. Defensive Actions:

Jumping spiders can react defensively by lifting their front legs, vibrating, or lunging when they feel threatened. Being aware of these defensive stances reduces needless tension during handling.

9. Recollection and Education:

It's thought that jumping spiders are intelligent and have good memories. They are able to recall precise locations, including those where they came across possible threats or prey. Their success as hunters is partly attributed to this cognitive ability.

10. Investigation of the Environment:

Because they are inquisitive, jumping spiders like to explore their surroundings. They might explore new things, move about their enclosure, or climb on things. Creating an environment that is stimulating encourages their innate curiosity.

11. Behavior in Territories:

Territorial behavior is something that jumping spiders may display, particularly during the mating season. Male spiders may guard particular regions in an effort to draw females for mating. Creating suitable spaces requires an understanding of territorial tendencies.

12. Mating and Procreation:

Spiders that jump perform intricate mating rituals. In order to entice females, male spiders frequently start courtship displays by showcasing their vivid colors and complex movements. Successful breeding requires an understanding of these rituals.

13. Acknowledgment of proprietors:

Some owners report that jumping spiders may exhibit signs of familiarity and recognition with their human caregivers, though the degree of this recognition is debatable. A trustworthy relationship is facilitated by positive and consistent interactions.

14. Positions for Rest:

The resting postures of jumping spiders are characteristic, as they frequently tuck their legs in close to their bodies. Seeing them in these positions can reveal information about how comfortable and content they are.

15. Individual Characteristics:

Every jumping spider might have different personalities and behaviors. While some people might be more cautious, others might be more daring. To provide your spider with more individualized care, pay attention to its unique habits and preferences.

You may build an environment that satisfies the physical and psychological demands of jumping spiders by comprehending these components of their behavior, which will result in an enriching and gratifying experience for both you and your arachnid partner.

CHAPTER 8

Tips for Breeding and Reproduction

Jumping spider breeding is an interesting endeavor. The following advice can assist you in navigating the process of breeding and reproduction:

1. Species Compatibility: Verify that the male and female jumping spiders are compatible. It's essential to comprehend the courtship rituals displayed by certain species in order to facilitate effective mating.

2. Pay Attention to Courtship Behaviors: Become acquainted with the ways that your particular species of jumping spider engages in courtship. In order to entice a possible partner, male jumping spiders frequently put on

elaborate displays that include vibrations and visual cues.

3. Introduce Mating Pairs: When you see responsive behaviors, introduce the male and female into a sharing enclosure. Keep a close eye on their interactions because courtship may be a complicated and time-consuming process.

4. Provide Enough Space: Make sure the breeding enclosure has enough room for interactions and wooing displays. To reduce stress and any disputes between mating pairs, try to avoid crowding.

5. Optimal Environmental Conditions: Preserve the ideal environmental conditions for mating and reproduction, including the right amounts of humidity and temperature. Examine the particular needs of your

species of jumping spider and try to recreate as much of their native environment as you can.

6. Provide Plenty of Live food: To guarantee that jumping spiders, both male and female, are well-fed before to and during the breeding process, provide a plentiful supply of live food. A healthy egg sac is more likely to be produced by a well-fed female.

7. Keep an Eye on the Female's Behavior: Pay close attention to the female's actions. Watch her for any indications of stress or hostility from the male after mating. To avoid harm, think about separating the couple if hostility is seen.

8. Construction of Egg Sacs: To protect their eggs, female jumping spiders build egg sacs. Give the female the right supplies, such silk threads, so she can make a safe egg

sac. Make sure she is in a calm and serene setting while doing this.

9. Incubation phase: Keep an eye on the incubation phase following the female's egg sac laying. Sustain consistent environmental conditions within the sac to facilitate the growth of spiderlings. For each species, the incubation period is different.

10. Provide Sufficient Ventilation: Make sure the enclosure containing the egg sac has enough ventilation. Enough ventilation is necessary to keep humidity levels stable, avoid mold growth, and provide a healthy environment for the spiderlings as they develop.

11. Be Ready for the Emergence of Spiderlings: Get ready for the appearance of spiderlings. After they hatch, they might go, so if you want to retain them, be

ready to take care of their needs or think about giving them a good home.

12. Divide the Spiderlings: To avoid cannibalism, if you plan to maintain the spiderlings, think about dividing them into separate enclosures. Provide suitable prey items and uphold ideal growth and development conditions for them.

13. Record the Breeding Process: Maintain thorough records of the mating dates, the development of the egg sacs, and the appearance of the spiderlings. If you ever want to share your breeding experiences with others, this paperwork may come in handy.

14. Consult Skilled Breeders: Ask arachnid aficionados or skilled jump spider breeders for help. Participate in internet communities or forums to share information

and gain insight from others who have successfully produced jumping spiders.

15. Exercise Patience and Observation: Raising jumping spiders takes both diligence and patience. Not every attempt will end in a successful mating, and knowing your species' natural habits is essential to make wise choices during the breeding process.

By using these pointers and paying close attention to your jumping spiders' distinct characteristics, you may increase the chances of a successful mating season and further knowledge and conservation of these fascinating arachnids.

Chapter 9

Do-It-Yourself Spider Enclosure Ideas

Building a homemade spider habitat can be a satisfying endeavor. The following ideas and actions will help you:

Supplies Required:

1. Container: Pick an airtight, transparent container. Glass or plastic containers are useful. Make sure the lid fits tightly to prevent escapes.

2. Substrate: Select a material to serve as the enclosing floor. For burrowing and webbuilding, coconut coir or a peat-based mixture makes an excellent foundation.

3. Decorative Elements: Include man-made or natural structures for hiding, climbing, and web attachment.

Artificial plants, silk anchor points, or small twigs can improve the setting.

4. Hiding locations: Use small shelters, cork bark, or other structures to create hiding locations. Your jumping spider can now withdraw and feel safe as a result.

5. Climbing Surfaces: Provide vertical components that facilitate climbing. When small branches or twigs are arranged vertically, your spider can display its innate tendency to climb.

6. Ventilation: Make sure the container has enough airflow by drilling holes in its top or sides. This keeps the atmosphere healthy and well-ventilated.

7. Temperature and Humidity Gauges: Install these gauges inside the enclosure to keep an eye on the

environment and modify it as needed to suit the requirements of your kind of jumping spider.

8. Water Dish: Provide a tiny, shallow dish for drinking water. Make sure the spider can reach it with ease and that it won't drown.

How to Make an Enclosure:

1. Clean the Container: Make sure the container you've chosen is completely free of any residue or impurities that could endanger your jumping spider.

2. Add Substrate: Add the chosen substrate to the bottom of the container. It should be deep enough for digging and web-building.

3. Arrange and Decorate the Elements: Include climbing structures, hiding places, and other accent pieces. Set

them up to give your leaping spider an eye-catching and engaging surroundings.

4. Ventilation Holes: Use a drill or a hot glue gun to make tiny ventilation holes. Make sure the openings are big enough to allow for sufficient airflow but small enough to prevent escape.

5. Position Climbing Surfaces: To satisfy the spider's innate inclinations, provide vertical climbing surfaces, like twigs or short branches, in strategic locations.

6. Install Water Dish: Set up the water dish in an enclosure corner. As a dependable source of water for your jumping spider, make sure it is sturdy and won't topple over.

7. Control of Temperature and Humidity: Place gauges to measure temperature and humidity in strategic places.

Adapt the enclosure's parameters to the needs of the species of your spider.

8. Tighten the Lid: Make sure there are no spaces in the lid that could allow air to escape. Put clamps or other safety precautions in place to keep the lid in place.

9. Introduce Your Spider: Gently acclimate your jumping spider to its new home after the enclosure has been assembled and the environment is stable. Keep an eye on its behavior to make sure it settles in securely.

10. Routine Maintenance: Create a schedule for routine maintenance. In order to create a wholesome and enriching living habitat, this involves cleaning, replacing substrate, and keeping an eye on environmental factors.

Ideas for Personalization:

Theme-Based Enclosures: Take into consideration designing enclosures with a theme based on the natural habitat of your jumping spider. Use appropriate décor to emulate particular ecosystems.

Investigate bioactive setups that include self-sustaining ecosystems, living plants, and microfauna—small helpful species. Before attempting a bioactive enclosure, do much research.

Using shelves or stacked containers, create multi tiered enclosures that offer vertical area for exploration and climbing.

instructional Displays: Create instructional displays that include labeled components that describe the characteristics and natural activities of jumping spiders.

Don't forget to investigate the particular requirements of your species of jumping spider and design the cage appropriately. Do-it-yourself endeavors allow you to express your creativity while putting your arachnid companion's health first.

Chapter 10

Typical Obstacles in the Care of Jumping Spiders

Although gratifying, caring for jumping spiders has its share of difficulties. The following are some typical obstacles and strategies for conquering them:

1. Managing Stress: Difficulty: When handled, jumping spiders may become anxious and exhibit protective tendencies.

Advice: Make handling sessions brief and sporadic. Keep an eye on their responses as you progressively foster trust via constructive encounters.

2. Attempts to Flee:

Challenge: Due to their agility, jumping spiders may try to get free while handling or when the enclosure is opened.

Advice: To reduce falls, handle your spider in close proximity to a sturdy surface. Use caution when opening the enclosure, and think about moving things around with catch cups.

3. Concerns about Molting:

Challenge: During the delicate period of molting, any perturbations may result in difficulties.

Advice: When molting, provide a calm and safe atmosphere. Steer clear of handling or significant enclosure modifications during this period.

4. Limited Accessibility to Particular Species:

Challenge: In some areas, certain species of jumping spiders might be less widespread or scarce.

Advice: Look into and select species that are easily found in your area. Consult respectable exotic pet retailers or breeders.

5. Prey Item Difficulties:

Challenge: It might be difficult to provide a steady supply of appropriate prey items, particularly for smaller spiderlings.

Advice: Grow fruit flies or other tiny insects to guarantee a consistent and suitable food supply. Think about the prey's size in comparison to the spider's size.

6. Health Issues: Difficulty: Health problems, such illnesses or injuries, might occur and need to be treated right once.

Advice: Keep a regular eye out for any indications of health issues with your jumping spider. If necessary, seek advice from a vet with experience treating exotic animals.

7. Unwanted Escapes: Difficulty: When the enclosure is opened or during routine maintenance, jumping spiders may unintentionally escape.

Advice: To reduce the possibility of escapes, maintain enclosures in a safe, enclosed area. When opening the enclosure, exercise caution.

8. Short Lifespan: Difficulty: Like many arachnids, jumping spiders have a comparatively short lifespan.

Advice: Recognize how long your particular species will live, and be ready to devote to the necessary time. Cherish and value every phase of their existence.

9. Territorial hostility: Difficulty: During the mating season in particular, territorial hostility might happen.

Advice: If you are keeping more than one spider, keep an eye on their behavior and be ready to take individual spiders apart if hostility arises. Give people plenty of room and places to hide.

10. Limited Resources for Veterinarians: Problem: It can be difficult to find a veterinarian who has experience with arachnids or exotic pets.

Connect with internet forums or communities where knowledgeable spider keepers can share their knowledge. Make a list of possible resources and conduct research on them for future reference.

11. Requirements Specific to Species:

Challenge: It can be difficult to meet the specific requirements of each species of jumping spider.

Research and comprehend the unique requirements of the species you have selected. Adjust the enclosure and maintenance procedures appropriately.

12. Variable Availability of Prey:

Problem: The range of prey items you can find may vary depending on where you are.

Advice: When possible, provide a variety of prey items to help diversify the diet. Think about substitutes such as premade fruit flies.

13. Limited Interaction: Difficulty: Establishing a rapport with jumping spiders can be difficult, and they might not be as interactive as some other pets.

Although not all jumping spiders are fun to handle, take some time to observe how they behave in the wild. Consistent grooming practices and a thoughtful enclosure foster bonding.

14. Educational Materials: Obstacle: It can be difficult to locate thorough and trustworthy information about caring for jumping spiders.

Investigate reliable internet discussion boards, arachnid care manuals, and related books. Speak with seasoned keepers to gain insightful knowledge.

15. Unpredictable Results of Mating:

Problem: Reproduction may not be successful in every try, and mating results are unpredictable.

Advice: Take note of observations and make adjustments after every breeding attempt. Successful mating is facilitated by knowing natural behaviors and having patience.

Through awareness of these obstacles and the application of deliberate care techniques, you can improve your jumping spider's health and successfully negotiate the pleasures and pitfalls of arachnid ownership.

Chapter 11

Considerations for Species-Specific Care

There are several species of jumping spiders, and each has special traits and needs for maintenance. The following are some general issues specific to each species:

1. The bold jumping spiders, Phidippus spp.

Features: Vibrant colors, substantial size, and sturdy construction.

Take Care: Make sure there is enough room for climbing and leaping. Known for their audacious demeanor, these spiders might tolerate handling better than certain other species.

2. Species of Jumping Spiders (Salticidae):

Features: a varied group that is frequently found in nature, exhibiting a range of colors and patterns.

Care Instructions: Provide a range of prey items for a balanced diet and create climbing surfaces that mimic their natural habitat.

3. The Ornate Jumping Spiders, Habronattus spp.

Features: Frequently identified by complex patterns and behaviors.

Taking Care of Things: Provide a setting that includes structures for web attachment and tiny hiding places. Observe how they respond to various pieces of prey.

4. Zebra Jumping Spiders, Euophrys spp.

Features: Easily recognizable patterns of black and white stripes.

Taking Care of Things: Give them climbing frames, and pay attention to how much room they require. Vertical components in their enclosure might be appreciated by these spiders.

5. The Lynx Jumping Spiders, or Marpissa spp.

Features: usually have longer bodies and are smaller in size.

Care Instructions: Provide an enclosure with hiding places and good ventilation. Compared to tropical species, lynx jumping spiders might prefer lower humidity levels.

6. Tropical Jumping Spiders, or Phintella spp., are distinguished by their vivid colors and frequent associations with tropical environments.

Taking Care of Things: To replicate their natural habitat, keep humidity levels higher and give a well-planted enclosure. Use ventilation carefully to avoid over-drying.

7. Menemerus Jumping Spiders, Plexippus spp.

Features: Slender build, a variety of colors and designs.

Taking Care of Things: Make an enclosure with climbing frames and provide a variety of food. Approach these spiders carefully as they may be more susceptible to manipulation.

8. Phiale spp., sometimes known as antlike jumping spiders: Features: resemble ants in appearance, as they frequently have distinct body forms.

Taking Care of Things: Provide vertical pieces and little hiding places. mimic the conditions of forest floors, which are their natural habitat.

The green coloring of the Marpissa muscosa (Green Jumping Spider) helps it blend in with the surrounding plants.

Care Instructions: Provide a lush, well-planted enclosure. It's possible that these spiders prefer conditions that imitate lush foliage.

10. Treedwelling Jumping Spiders (Maevia spp.): Features slim body, suited for dwelling in trees.

Taking Care of Things: Provide climbing features that are vertical, and make sure the lid is tight to stop escapes. It's possible that these spiders like higher spots in their cage.

11. Slender jumping spiders, or Saitis spp.

Features: Slender, long bodies, frequently with mysterious coloring.

Taking Care of Things: Provide concealing and climbing structures. Observe how sensitive they are to environmental changes.

12. Feather-legged jumping spiders, or Pystira spp.

Features: known for having leg structures that resemble feathers.

Taking Care of Things: Make sure the enclosure has enough places for climbing. During courtship, feather legged jumping spiders may display unusual behaviors.

13. Sun-jumping spiders, Heliophanus spp.:

Features: Widely differing in size and color, frequently linked to sunny locations.

Taking Care of Things: Provide climbing structures and a well-lit area. Observe how they respond to various lighting situations.

14. Characteristics of transparent jumping spiders, Lyssomanes spp. renowned for having bodies that are translucent, which makes interior components remarkably visible.

Taking Care of Things: Keep a hiding place and an enclosure with good ventilation. During their molting process, transparent jumping spiders could be vulnerable to disruptions.

15. Springtime Jumping Spiders, or Evarcha spp.

Qualities: Quick-witted and agile in movement.

Care Instructions: Provide a roomy cage with mechanisms for quick motions. Take into account a bigger arrangement to satisfy their energetic nature.

Always learn the particular maintenance needs of the species of jumping spider you choose to maintain. For a fruitful and satisfying keeping experience, adjust the enclosure's layout, temperature, humidity, and feeding procedures according to the natural environment and habits of the selected species.

Chapter 12

Improving the Environment for Leaping Spiders

Enhancing the environment is essential to supporting jumping spider health and natural habits. The following are some methods to improve your arachnid companion's surroundings:

1. Climbing Structures: Include vertical components such as twigs or tiny branches. Because they are innate climbers, jumping spiders can display their activities on these structures.

2. Artificial Plants: Use fake plants to resemble greenery. These not only improve the enclosure's aesthetic appeal but also provide hiding places and web attachment anchor points.

3. Hiding Spots: Construct little shelters out of half-coconut shells or cork bark. These concealing places promote natural behaviors like retreat and observation while also providing protection.

4. Variety of Substrate: To generate a range of textures, use a variety of substrates. Use materials like as peat, sphagnum moss, and coconut coir to replicate the various ground textures that they might encounter in their natural environments.

5. Live Plants (If Suitable): If the species of your spider allows, think about putting some live plants in the cage. Some jumping spiders prefer areas with live foliage because it gives them more hiding places and a more organic look.

6. Silk Anchor Points: Stitch tiny silk anchor points all throughout the cage. Silk threads serve a variety of

functions for jumping spiders, and these anchor points let them construct makeshift lairs or passageways.

7. Variety of Prey things: Provide a range of prey things. Try experimenting with several insect species to simulate the variety of food that jumping spiders would come across in the wild. This satisfies their hunting instincts in addition to providing nourishment.

8. Changing the décor: Rearrange the décor pieces from time to time. This keeps their surroundings interesting and piques the spiders' curiosity. Make sure adjustments are made gradually to prevent tension.

9. Modifiable illumination: Modify the illumination according to the type of spider. While certain species could do well in brighter illumination, others might do better in more muted settings. Emulating the rhythms of natural illumination enhances their health.

10. Establish safe observation areas: Set up areas for safe observation close to the enclosure. This gives you the opportunity to watch your jumping spider without having to handle it directly, stimulating your mind without making you stressed.

11. Reflection Mirrors: Place little mirrors outside the fence. According to some owners, jumping spiders find cerebral stimulation in staring at their own reflections.

12. Interactive Feeders: To keep the spider interested while it is feeding, use interactive feeders. Move the prey items slowly across the enclosure to encourage the spider to hunt and engage in its natural activities.

13. Regular Enclosure Cleaning: Conduct routine enclosure cleanings. Eliminating leftover food, molts, and keeping things clean helps to create a healthy

atmosphere and reduce stress brought on by unhygienic surroundings.

14. Background Images: Adhere artwork or background pictures to the enclosure's outside. This improves overall aesthetics by adding visual interest and possibly achieving a more realistic image.

15. Soft Sounds: Add soft sounds to the spider's surroundings. Although they lack typical ears, spiders are nevertheless able to hear vibrations. A more stimulating atmosphere could be enhanced by soothing background noise.

Understanding the habits and preferences of your jumping spider is essential for effective environmental enrichment. Try varying things and see how your spider reacts. Then, make necessary adjustments to the container. Encouraging and varied surroundings are beneficial to your spider friend's general health.

Chapter 13: Legal and Ethical Aspects of Spider Keeping

Responsible ownership of spiders is ensured by taking certain legal and ethical aspects into account. Here are some important things to remember:

1. Legal Requirements: Verify the national, state, and municipal laws governing the ownership of spiders. Certain species might be protected, and permissions might be needed to own them. Make sure you abide by all relevant laws.

2. Protected Species: Take note of any spiders that are designated as endangered or protected. Unauthorized taking or possession of these animals may have legal repercussions and have a detrimental effect on conservation efforts.

3. Invading Species: Steer clear of harboring invading organisms. Negro species can have negative impacts on regional ecosystems when they are introduced into the environment. One aspect of responsible ownership is keeping non-native spiders from escaping or being released.

4. Ethical Sourcing: Use responsible and ethical methods to source spiders. Buy spiders from reliable sellers or breeders who put the health of the animals first. Refrain from endorsing the illicit trafficking in wildlife.

5. Knowledge and Education: Get knowledgeable about the particular requirements and habits of the spider species you choose to raise. A part of responsible ownership is giving the right treatment based on correct information.

6. Conservation Considerations: Take into account the species' current state of conservation. Make sure your activities support conservation efforts when you care for a threatened or endangered species. Steer clear of aiding the trafficking in threatened species.

7. Responsibly Breeding: If you breed, make sure to do so in an ethical manner. Make sure that the breeding process benefits the health of the species and refrain from unneeded or detrimental procedures.

8. Preventing Overpopulation: Take note of any possible problems related to overpopulation. Managing reproduction to avoid unforeseen effects, such overcrowding or trouble finding acceptable homes for kids, is part of responsible ownership.

9. Appropriate Containment Maintenance: To stop escapes, keep enclosures in good condition. In the

environment, stray spiders could endanger local species or spread like invasive plants. Employ safe containers with tightly fitted covers.

10. Preventing Injury to Humans: Take into account any possible risks to people, particularly if you own poisonous animals. Prevent unintentional bites using safety measures, and be ready to seek medical assistance if needed. Inform your family members about any hazards.

11. Dispelling Myths: Dispel common assumptions and folklore around spiders. Promoting accurate information about spiders to allay anxieties and advance conservation initiatives is part of responsible ownership.

12. Humane therapy: Adopt a humane approach to therapy. Avoid needless tension by treating spiders with

kindness and care. Assure adequate nourishment and provide livable conditions.

13. Collaboration and Communication: Talk to other enthusiasts and keepers. Participate in communities or forums where you may exchange best practices, insights, and experiences. Working together helps us understand spider care better.

14. Public Perception: Pay attention to how the public perceives you. Although raising spiders can be a fulfilling pastime, some people may be wary of it. Inform people on the value and significance of spiders in ecosystems.

15. Personal Safety: Give your own safety first priority. Recognize the possible dangers of working with particular species. When necessary, exercise caution and take precautionary steps.

Legal observance, moral principles, and a dedication to the welfare of the creatures are all part of responsible spider keeping. Remain knowledgeable, never stop learning, and make a constructive contribution to the preservation and comprehension of these amazing arachnids.

BONUS CHAPTER

FAQS

1. What species of spiders jump?

The main food source for jumping spiders is tiny insects like ants, mosquitoes, and flies.

2. Do jumping spiders have a long jumping distance?

Indeed, jumping spiders are renowned for their remarkable leaping prowess, reaching heights many times greater than their body length.

3. Do spiders that jump weave webs?

Although jumping spiders don't make conventional webs to capture food, they do employ silk for draglines and escapes.

4. Are humans poisoned by jumping spiders?

Although jumping spiders can sting, humans are not harmed by their venom. Their bites rarely hurt and don't do much damage.

5. What is the lifespan of jumping spiders?
Jumping spiders can live anywhere from a few months to a year, depending on the species.

6. Do jumping spiders know who owns them?
Although specialists disagree about the depth of their observations, some owners claim that their jumping spiders may exhibit symptoms of familiarity and awareness.

7. Do jumping spiders enjoy being touched?
Although this varies from person to person, many jumping spiders respond well to gentle, infrequent handling.

8. Is it possible for jumping spiders to coexist in the same enclosure?

Since jumping spiders live alone most of the time, living together can result in territorial conflicts. It's safest to store them apart.

9. How often do molts occur in jumping spiders?

In order to grow, jumping spiders molt on occasion. Age and species are two characteristics that affect the frequency.

10. Are jumping spiders able to see well?

It's true that jumping spiders have good vision; in particular, their huge anterior median eyes allow them to track prey accurately.

11. Can people keep jumping spiders as pets?

Indeed, a lot of individuals own jumping spiders as pets because of their interesting habits and cheap maintenance requirements.

12. What size enclosure is necessary for jumping spiders?

The size of the enclosure varies by species, but most jumping spiders can be housed in a tiny container with climbing mechanisms.

13. Are jumping spiders heat-sensitive?

The majority of jumping spiders can survive at room temperature, but a stable and cozy habitat is necessary.

14. Can store-bought insects be fed to jumping spiders?

Indeed, a range of store-bought insects, such as fruit flies, crickets, and tiny moths, can be given to jumping spiders.

15. How do spiders that jump communicate?

During courtship rituals, jumping spiders use vibrations, visual displays, and silk thread communication to convey their messages.

16. What is the jumping spider's mating behavior?

Male jumping spiders frequently perform complex displays of courtship that include complicated movements, vibrations, and occasionally the gifting of prey.

17. Are jumping spiders able to identify their prey at a distance?

Indeed, jumping spiders' keen vision allows them to identify possible prey from a distance, which helps them in their hunting tactics.

18. How do spiders that jump hunt?

To catch prey, jumping spiders use stalking and leaping techniques. A crucial component of their hunting method is their ability to jump precisely.

19. Are jumping spiders an excellent pet for education?
Indeed, jumping spiders can make interesting educational pets that teach about the ways of arachnids and the natural world.

20. Do leaping spiders pose a threat?
Humans are not in risk from jumping spiders. They are normally gentle, and their poison is mild. Bites are uncommon and seldom harmful.

21. Are colonies or groups of jumping spiders possible to keep?
No, jumping spiders are solitary animals, and housing them in groups could lead to stress and territorial problems.

22. What is the everyday use of silk for jumping spiders?
Silk is used by jumping spiders for a variety of tasks, such as making egg sacs, retreats, and draglines for protection.

23. What indicate a healthy jumping spider might have?
A healthy jumping spider will move around a lot, seem well-groomed, and have a steady appetite for prey.

24. Are there any specific humidity requirements for jumping spiders?
Although species-specific humidity requirements can differ, many jumping spiders thrive under moderate humidity conditions. It is essential to investigate your spider's particular requirements.

25. How can leaping spiders fend off would-be attackers?

In order to protect themselves, jumping spiders can move swiftly and erratically, jump far away from danger, and use camouflage to fit in with their environment.

26. Can jumping spiders distinguish between several human faces?

Some jumping spiders may be able to distinguish between distinct human faces, according to research.

27. Are there any particular jumping spider breeds that are suggested for novices?

For novices, Phidippus spp.—also referred to as courageous jumping spiders—are frequently suggested because of their resilience and captivating nature.

28. If my jumping spider won't eat, what should I do?

Observe the spider for indications of stress or disease. If the refusal doesn't go away, think about changing the enclosure's settings, providing an alternative prey item, or speaking with knowledgeable caretakers.

29. Are male and female jumping spiders different in color?

There may be color variations between men and females in some species. During mating season, males may display more vivid colors or different patterns.

30. Is it possible to house jumping spiders in an open terrarium?

Even while jumping spiders don't typically climb like many arboreal species do, escapes are still a possibility in an open terrarium. Using a tight-fitting lid on a secure container is advised.

31. Are there any telltale symptoms that my jumping spider is about to shed its skin?

A reduction in activity, color changes, and the spider constructing a tiny silk mat or retreating are all indicators that a molt is about to occur.

32. Can one train a leaping spider?

Some owners say that jumping spiders can respond to certain cues and even grow accustomed to good interactions, even though typical training methods may not work with them.

33. How long do jumping spiderlings live?

Although spiderling lifespans vary by species, they usually reach adulthood between a few weeks to several months.

34. How can spiders that jump breathe?

The respiratory organ known as book lungs, which is present in jumping spiders, enables them to take in oxygen from the atmosphere.

35. Can a jumping spider and another pet share a room?
Even though jumping spiders are usually harmless and low care, it's important to protect other pets as well as the spiders themselves. Keep enclosures safe and keep an eye on interactions.

36. Are there any particular health problems that jumping spiders frequently face?
Common health problems could be caused by stress, difficulties with molting, or problems with unsuitable environmental circumstances. It is essential to conduct routine observation in order to identify and manage possible health problems.

37. What part does silk play in the courtship rituals of jumping spiders?
During their courtship displays, male jumping spiders use silk to create intricate structures or vibrations that

entice females. Certain animals employ silk to visually communicate with prospective partners.

38. Do jumping spiders have night vision?

Despite having great vision, jumping spiders are not meant to see in total darkness. They depend on their vision, especially in areas with good lighting.

39. How do jumping spiders adjust to environmental changes?

Although jumping spiders can adapt to variations in humidity, temperature, and illumination, abrupt or drastic changes may stress them out.

40. Do jumping spiders go through stressful times?

Indeed, stress can be experienced by jumping spiders, particularly in response to harsh handling, loud noises, or environmental changes. Reducing stressors is crucial for their well-being.

41. Is it possible to breed jumping spiders in groups?

A male and female may be temporarily housed together in order to breed jumping spiders, but it's crucial to keep a tight eye on their interactions to avoid any potential harm.

42. How do jumping spiders prepare for mating?

With the help of their unique mouthparts and legs, jumping spiders clean their bodies and get rid of any trash or foreign objects.

43. Exist any particular signs that my jumping spider is under stress?

Jumping spiders may exhibit unpredictable behavior, decreased activity, color changes, and food avoidance as indicators of stress.

44. For enclosures containing jumping spiders, what kind of substrate is appropriate?

For jumping spider enclosures, substrates like coconut coir, sphagnum moss, or a combination of peat and vermiculite are frequently utilized because they offer an appropriate surface for burrowing.

45. Can different types of prey be recognized by jumping spiders?

Diverse prey items can be distinguished by jumping spiders, who may exhibit preference depending on attributes such as size, mobility, or other characteristics.

46. How can I give my jumping spider a realistic habitat?

To replicate the natural habitat of the spider, use a variety of artificial or live plants, climbing frames, and appropriate planting material. Think about the particular requirements of your kind of spider.

47. Exist any particular warning indicators prior to a jumping spider bite?

Typically, jumping spiders don't show any symptoms prior to biting. Nevertheless, bites are uncommon, and humans are not significantly affected medically by their venom.

48. Are jumping spiders able to identify themselves or other spiders?

Although the degree of identification varies, some jumping spiders may exhibit interest toward other spiders or even their own reflection.

49. Without a web, how do jumping spiders hunt?

Jumping spiders hunt and pounce on victims using their acute vision and dexterity. They may employ silk for safety and communication instead of relying solely on webs for hunting.

50. What safety measures ought to I use when working with jumping spiders?

To prevent stress, handle jumping spiders sparingly and with gentle handling. Recognize their stature and dexterity to avoid unintentional escapes. Before and after handling, wash your hands.

51. Can spiders that jump distinguish between different human voices?

Though it's unclear if they can identify distinct human voices, jumping spiders might be perceptive to noises and sensations in their surroundings.

52. How can I determine my jumping spider's gender?

Males of certain species may be smaller and have more vivid colors. Especially during the breeding season, females may appear larger and have a more robust abdomen.

53. Do jumping spiders shed their skin in several pieces or just one?

Usually, jumping spiders molt in several sections. They exoskeleton sheds in pieces, the abdomen coming off first and then the cephalothorax.

54. Are jumping spiders able to detect sound?
Despite without having ears, jumping spiders are able to hear and feel vibrations in their environment, which gives them the ability to detect sounds and movement.

55. Can invertebrates be kept in the same home as jumping spiders?
House jumping spiders shouldn't be kept with other invertebrates because of the unexpected nature of their interactions, which might result in fights.

56. What does the male jumping spider dance represent in terms of courtship?
The male jumping spiders use their courtship dance to draw in the females. It entails complex motions, eye-

catching displays, and occasionally giving the female a gift of prey.

57. Are jumping spiders exhibiting any particular symptoms of disease?

Illness symptoms can include fatigue, trouble moving, color changes, or strange behaviors. If you notice any worrying indicators, get advice from knowledgeable keepers or an exotic pet veterinarian.

58. How can I help my jumping spider to construct a cocoon?

If you give a jumping spider the right supplies, such as fine silk strands or anchor points inside the enclosure, it will build silk retreats.

59. Is it possible to keep jumping spiders in bioactive setups with living plants?

Although some keepers have constructed effective bioactive settings, it is important to carefully evaluate the requirements of the plants employed and the unique demands of the species of jumping spiders.

60. How do clean jumpers keep that way?

Using unique bristles on their legs, jumping spiders clean and remove dirt and debris from their bodies on a regular basis.

61. Do jumping spiders make "parachutes" out of silk to help them travel?

By releasing silk threads that catch the wind, certain jumping spiders can move short distances—a process called "ballooning."

62. Do jumping spiders have the ability to solve problems?

According to research, jumping spiders can solve difficulties by figuring out how to get around barriers and locate the quickest paths to their food.

63. Are jumping spiders able to see under UV light?

It has been shown that jumping spiders are sensitive to UV light, which may help them communicate and locate prey.

64. Are jumping spiders individuals?

It has been suggested by some researchers that jumping spiders might have unique personalities, exhibiting differences in behavior and reactions to stimuli.

65. What does it mean when some jumping spiders have iridescent scales?

Some jumping spiders have iridescent scales that could be used as visual cues during courtship, providing information about the genetic fitness and general health of the spider.

66. Are jumping spiders known to resemble and behave like ants?

Certain jumping spiders imitate the appearance and behavior of ants, a tactic they use to evade predators.

67. How do "footflagging" jumping spiders communicate?

Jumping spiders perform a technique called footflagging in which they wave their legs or pedipalps in predetermined patterns. It is believed that this conduct contributes to communication throughout the courtship phase.

68. Are jumping spiders able to identify and react to variations in human emotions?

There is evidence that jumping spiders can recognize changes in human facial expressions and respond appropriately, though the exact level of this ability is still unknown.

69. Do jumping spiders have a niche where they hunt other spiders?

Certain jumping spiders seek spiders specifically, feeding on other spiders. To get closer, they could imitate the vibrations of a spider that is stuck.

70. How do jumping spiders go across challenging environments?

To travel precisely through intricate terrain, jumping spiders employ a combination of tactile sense through their leg hairs and vision.

71. Are leaping spiders temporally aware?

Some research indicates that jumping spiders might have an internal sense of time that influences their actions, though this is yet unclear.

72. Can spiders that jump detect their own reflections?

Research has shown that some jumping spiders are able to identify their own reflections and react aggressively or curiously to the picture that they see.

73. How do vibratory signals get communicated among jumping spiders?

Jumping spiders add a dimension to their social interactions by using vibrations as a kind of communication. These vibrations can carry information about territorial boundaries, aggressiveness, or courting.

74. Do jumping spiders have any territoriality?

Numerous jumping spiders are territorial in nature, guarding particular regions that offer resources like prey and possible mates.

75. What function does leaping spiders' "semaphore" activity serve?

Certain jumping spiders display semaphore behavior, whereby they communicate by making particular leg movements that may indicate their intentions.

76. Can jumping spiders change their hunting tactics according to the availability of prey?

According to research, jumping spiders exhibit adaptable behaviors by adjusting their hunting techniques according to the availability of various prey items.

77. How are the eyes of jumping spiders cleaned?

In order to maintain the best vision possible for hunting and navigating their surroundings, jumping spiders use specialized bristles on their legs to clean their primary eyes.

78. Are there any jumping spiders that copy the courtship rituals of other spider species?

Some jumping spiders exhibit a sort of deceitful behavior by imitating the courtship rituals of other spider species in order to approach and mate with females.

79. Are jumping spiders able to distinguish between different colors?

According to studies, jumping spiders are able to discriminate between colors, and certain species may have color preferences that affect which partners or prey they choose.

80. What role does UV reflectance play in jumping spiders' courting displays?

During mating displays, some jumping spiders use UV reflectance patterns on their bodies. These patterns may not be apparent to humans, yet they are an essential part of spider communication.

81. What use does jumping spiders' "tap dancing" activity serve?

Certain jumping spiders make rhythmic vibrations by tapping their legs on a surface, a technique known as tap dancing. It is believed that this conduct is connected to courting or communication.

82. Are jumping spiders able to identify certain humans?

According to research, jumping spiders may be able to identify distinct individuals and respond differently depending on their prior interactions.

83. In what ways do jumping spiders use problem-solving skills to hunt?

When hunting, jumping spiders demonstrate their ability to solve issues by calculating the length and direction of their jumps in order to successfully catch prey.

84. Do jumping spiders construct intricate nests?

Certain jumping spiders create elaborate silk nests that feature compartments and barriers to keep out predators, demonstrating highly developed silkspinning techniques.

85. Can jumping spiders learn up knowledge by watching other spiders?

According to studies, jumping spiders exhibit a degree of social learning by being able to pick up skills from watching the activities of conspecifics, or other spiders of their same species.

86. What does "leg waving" mean in the language of jumping spiders?

Jumping spiders use their leg movements to communicate with each other in a rhythmic manner. During encounters, this behavior could reveal information about their objectives.

87. Can jumping spiders tell the difference between several kinds of silk threads?

Spiders that jump are able to distinguish between different types of silk threads and can identify the distinctive qualities of strands used for retreats or draglines, for example.

88. What role do tactile cues play in jumping spider courtship?

In jumping spider courtship, individuals use tactile cues to identify potential mates and communicate, such as leg touches or vibrations.

89. Exist any jumping spider species that engages in cooperative hunting?

Some jumping spiders exhibit cooperative hunting, a social activity in which several individuals cooperate to catch larger prey.

90. Why do jumping spiders engage in "mirroring" behavior?

Spiders that engage in mirrored behavior will jump to imitate the actions of a potential partner. Courtship rituals are supposed to involve this coordinated conduct.

91. Are jumping spiders able to identify particular landmarks in their surroundings?

It's possible that jumping spiders may identify and make use of particular landmarks in their environment for direction and navigation.

92. How is silk used by jumping spiders as a safety line when they jump?

Jumping spiders deploy silk threads as safety lines during long jumps. They can easily climb back up using the silk thread if the jump doesn't work.

93. Do any jumping spiders imitate other species' mating signals in order to trick prospective partners?

By mimicking the mating signals of other spider species, several jumping spiders engage in aggressive mimicry, deceiving prospective partners into approaching.

94. What role do vibrations in the abdomen play in jumping spider communication?

It is thought that during courtship or territorial encounters, jumping spiders that move their abdomen rhythmically transmit extra information.

95. Are jumping spiders able to distinguish between vibrations from their prey and background noise?

Vibrations from possible prey and significant social interactions are the vibrations that jumping spiders are able to selectively select out of their environment.

96. How can jumping spiders move across surfaces that are upside down?

Because of the unique adhesive setae on their legs, jumping spiders can easily cling to and move across inverted surfaces.

97. Exist any jumping spiders that resemble ants in both look and behavior?

In order to avoid being seen by predators, certain jumping spiders replicate activities other than visual mimicry, such as moving in an antlike manner.

98. How can jumping spiders construct "paratrooper" lines out of silk for protection?

Some jumping spiders release silk while they fall, creating "paratrooper" lines in addition to ballooning. This aids in their safe landing by slowing their descent.

99. Are jumping spiders able to identify particular forms or patterns?

Research indicates that jumping spiders may be cognitively capable due to their capacity to identify particular patterns or forms.

BONDING STRATEGY

1. Observation Time: Spend some peaceful time monitoring your jumping spider to better understand its behavior.

2. Gentle Handling Sessions: Introduce gentle handling sessions gradually to let your spider become accustomed to your presence.

3. Consistent Feeding pattern: - To generate a good association, establish a consistent feeding pattern.

4. Create a Comfortable Habitat: - Provide a comfortable and well-designed enclosure that closely resembles the spider's natural habitat.

5. Incorporate secure Hiking locations: Include secure hiding locations within the enclosure for your spider to flee to when necessary.

6. Use Calm and Slow Movements: - To avoid stress, move gently and quietly around your spider.

7. Positive Reinforcement with Treats: During encounters, offer treats, such as little insects, as positive reinforcement.

8. Avoid abrupt Loud Noises: - Keep abrupt loud noises to a minimum, as they may scare your jumping spider.

9. Introduce New Enclosure Additions progressively: - To avoid stress, introduce new enclosure elements progressively.

10. Establish a Regular Handling Schedule: - Create a regular handling schedule to increase familiarity.

11. Imitate Natural Lighting Conditions: Attempt to replicate natural lighting conditions in order to encourage a normal day-night cycle.

12. Use a Textured Substrate: - Select a substrate with a texture ideal for burrowing and web creation.

13. Rotate Enrichment Items: - To keep the environment interesting, rotate toys or climbing structures.

14. Include Silk Anchor Points: - Silk anchor points are included to stimulate web-building behavior.

15. Provide Climbing Options: Include vertical features for climbing and exploring.

16. Experiment with Various Food varieties: - Experiment with different insect varieties to establish your spider's preferences.

17. Use a Soft Brush for Grooming: - Gently groom with a soft brush, emulating natural actions.

18. Create a Webbing Area: - Within the enclosure, choose a location for web development.

19. Observe Molting Behaviors: Observe molting behaviors and avoid needless disruptions.

20. Include Artificial or Live Plants: For further enrichment, include artificial or live plants.

21. Temperature Monitoring: Observe and maintain appropriate temperature conditions.

22. Offer a Variety of Climbing Structures: - Provide a variety of climbing structures for physical activities.

23. Create a midday Routine: - Create a midday routine to give predictability.

24. Interactive Laser Pointers: For movement, gently engage your spider with an interactive laser pointer.

Silk Thread for Exploration: Tie silk threads to safe anchor points for exploration.

26. Play Gentle Music: During periods of interaction, play soft and calming music.

27. Custom Hideouts: For variation, create custom hideouts with varied textures.

28. Regular Health exams: Perform regular health exams to monitor general health.

29. Observe Web creation: Observe and enjoy the web creation process.

30. Design a bespoke Water Dish: - Create a bespoke water dish for easy hydration.

31. Experiment with Different Substrates: - Experiment with different substrates to determine which one your spider prefers.

32. Silk Bridge Construction: - Create silk bridges to connect climbing structures.

33. Provide Unique Climbing tasks: Create climbing tasks with varied levels of difficulty.

34. Natural Light Exposure: Allow for natural light exposure without direct sunlight.

35. Interactive Laser Maze: Design an interactive laser maze for your spider to explore.

36. Use delicate Touch for Interaction: - To avoid stress, use a delicate touch when handling.

37. Rotate Enclosure arrangement: For variety, rotate the enclosure arrangement on a regular basis.

38. Create a Warmth Gradient: - Create a temperature gradient within the enclosure.

39. Web upkeep Monitoring: Observe and assist with web upkeep as needed.

40. Vary Prey Sizes: - Vary prey sizes to ensure a diversified diet.

41. Provide Small Mirrors: - Provide small mirrors to examine the reactions of your spider.

42. Temperature Gradient for Basking: Include a temperature gradient to provide possibilities for basking.

43. Build a Miniature Jungle Gym: - Create a miniature jungle gym for climbing activities.

44. Create a Tactile Exploration Zone: - Set up a tactile exploration zone with varied textures.

45. Play soothing Nature Sounds: During peaceful times, play soothing nature sounds.

46. Observe Hunting Strategies: Observe and admire your spider's distinct hunting techniques.

47. Experiment with Different Web Designs: Allow your spider to experiment with different web designs.

48. Photography Sessions: Invest in photography sessions to capture your spider's development.

49. Provide Elevated Vantage spots: - Provide elevated observation spots.

50. Include a Small Water Feature: - Include a small water feature for enhanced sensory stimulation.

51. Silk Thread Art Display: Allow your spider to make silk thread art as a one-of-a-kind display.

display.

52. Make a Natural Hideaway: - Make natural hideaways out of rocks or bark.

53. Variable Light Intensity: Experiment with different light intensities during the day and at night.

54. Misting Sessions: Use misting sessions to regulate humidity.

55. Incorporate Rotating Insect odors: Introduce rotating insect odors to enhance hunting behaviors.

Tiny Mirrored Disco Ball: - For reflecting play, place a tiny mirrored disco ball.

57. Attach Hanging sweets: - For interactive feeding, hang sweets with silk threads.

58. Plan a Spider "Treasure Hunt": Arrange sweets strategically for a spider "treasure hunt."

59. Spider-Safe Herb Garden: For sensory experiences, grow a spider-safe herb garden.

bespoke Climbing Obstacle Course: Create a bespoke climbing obstacle course using a variety of surfaces.

61. Silk Thread Bridge Challenges: Build silk thread bridges of varied heights and lengths.

62. Make a Web Repair Kit: - Keep a modest kit on hand to aid with web repairs if necessary.

63. Feeding Puzzles: Use feeding puzzles to encourage mental engagement.

64. Silk Thread Art Display Wall: Make a wall specifically for showing silk thread art.

65. bespoke-Designed Enclosure backdrops: Create bespoke enclosure backdrops.

66. Incorporate Safe Floral Additions: - For visual flair, add spider-safe flowers.

67. Rotate Artificial Foliage: For environmental enrichment, rotate artificial foliage on a regular basis.

68. Spider-Safe Live Plants: Include spider-safe live plants for a natural touch.

69. Custom Webbing Frames: Create frames to display your spider's beautiful webbing.

70. Explore Portable Playpens: Use portable playpens outside the enclosure for supervised exploration.

71. Seasonal Enclosure Themes: For diversity, create seasonal themes within the enclosure.

72. Spider-Safe Aromatherapy: Use moderate smells for spider-safe aromatherapy.

73. Bubble Wrap Popping Sessions: Occasionally provide bubble wrap for popping pleasure.

74. Spider-Safe Hanging Hammock: Make a peaceful hanging silk hammock.

75. Spider-Safe Vibrating Toys: Provide tactile stimulation with spider-safe vibrating toys.

Spider "Obstacle Course" Challenges: Create an obstacle course to test your spider's agility.

77. Rotate Spider-Safe Climbing Plants: - For diversity, rotate spider-safe climbing plants.

78. Spider-Safe Terrarium Stickers: Decorate your enclosure with terrarium stickers.

79. Custom Spider Playhouse: Construct a little playhouse within the confines of the cage.

80. Spider-Safe Wind Chimes: Place spider-safe wind chimes about the house for auditory stimulation.

81. Spider-Safe Light-Up Toys: Use light-up toys for visual stimulation.

82. Spider-Safe Puzzle Feeders: - Provide spider-safe puzzle feeders to keep your mind stimulated.

83. Spider-Safe Feathered Toys: For tactile play, introduce spider-safe feathered toys.

84. Spider-Safe little Ladder: Include a little ladder for adventurous climbing.

85. Spider-Safe Puzzle Boxes: Store snacks in spider-proof puzzle boxes.

86. Spider-Safe Small Mirrors: - Introduce small mirrors for exploring.

87. Spider-Safe Rotating Mirrored Disco Ball: - Install a rotating mirrored disco ball for visual pleasure.

88. Spider-Safe little Jungle Gym: - Create a little jungle gym for climbing and exploration.

89. Spider-Safe Interactive Projector Games: - Use interactive projector games for visual engagement.

90. Spider-Safe UV Light: - Incorporate a spider-safe UV light for increased visibility.

91. Spider-Safe Bouncy Toys: - Use spider-safe bouncy toys for play.

92. Spider-Safe little Swing: - Include a little swing for swinging enjoyment.

93. Spider-Safe Texture Panels: - Add textured panels for tactile pleasures.

94. Spider-Safe spinning Perch: - Install a spinning perch for dynamic climbing.

95. Spider-Safe Puzzle Rugs: - Place rewards in spider-safe puzzle rugs.

96. Spider-Safe Rolling Toys: - Use spider-safe rolling toys for exploration.

97. Spider-Safe Floating Platforms: - Create floating platforms for novel climbing options.

98. Spider-Safe Chirping Toy: - Introduce a spider-safe chirping toy for auditory stimulation.

99. Spider-Safe Climbing Nets: - Install spider-safe climbing nets for added vertical space.

100. Spider-Safe Hanging Bridge: - Create a spider-safe hanging bridge for dynamic movement.

These tactics provide a broad range of activities to engage and bond with your jumping spider while encouraging physical and cerebral stimulation in a safe and enriching setting. Remember to watch your spider's preferences and alter activities accordingly for a happy and healthy pet experience.

Made in the USA
Coppell, TX
03 January 2025